HOW TO STUDY
THE BIBLE, PART I

HOW TO STUDY
THE BIBLE, PART I

LAY ACTION MINISTRY PROGRAM
7200 E. DRY CREEK ROAD, SUITE D-202
ENGLEWOOD, CO 80112

93 92 91 90 89   5   4   3   2

David C. Cook Publishing Co.
850 North Grove Avenue
Elgin, IL 60120
Printed in U.S.A.

Editor: Gary Wilde
Designer: Chris Patchel
Cover: Lois Rosio Sprague

ISBN: 0-89191-516-8
Library of Congress Catalog Number: 86-72600

TABLE OF
CONTENTS

ACKNOWLEDGMENTS

How to Study the Bible was developed with the conviction that many lay people want to study the Bible more effectively, and with greater benefit. Many would also like to use what they have learned and experienced in ministry to others.

In writing this study course, LAMP is grateful for the considerable preliminary work done by Dr. Earl McQuay. We are also very grateful for the numerous suggestions that improved the text. Some were made by those who initially reviewed the material, and many others by those who either taught, or studied the course in its three separate text stages. Among these are: Wilfred Gunderson, William Schmalgemeier, Paul Renovitch, Robert Sutherland, Robert Maitan, Jane Neuvirth, John Rynders, Bruce Youngquist, Warren Cheek, Lowell Friesen, David Lanoha, Tom Lambelet, David Freitag and Laverne McFarland.

For Scripture quotations, the New American Standard Bible was chosen both because of the extensive cross-references found in the NASB study edition and because the literal rendering of the original languages makes it a good choice for serious Bible study.

Dr. Robert L. Samms
January 28, 1985

LAY ACTION
MINISTRY PROGRAM

LAMP courses are based on the HEAD, HEART, and HANDS approach to learning. HEAD represents Bible _content_ that you want to know. HEART represents your _personal application_ of the truth. HANDS refers to the LAMP goal of preparing you to _use course content in the lives of other people_—imparting to others what you have learned (see II Tim. 2:2).

How to Study the Bible can be the finest Bible study experience of your life. If you diligently study each lesson, the course can make you a careful student of Scripture, and a confident Bible study leader.

Course Requirements

This course is for every Christian who is willing to put forth the effort in personal study. But we want you to know "up front" what it is going to cost you in terms of time and commitment. First, _it is going to cost you a good hour of home study for each lesson._ Make every effort to spend this much time as a minimum requirement.

Second, this course will cost you the price of a number of essential reference books. (These reference tools are covered in Lesson 2.) You may be able to borrow some of them, but if you buy them you can use them throughout your life, in study and ministry. You will need to use these study tools weekly in order to complete parts I and II of _How to Study the Bible._

How to Use This Course

Though you may complete the course by yourself, you will normally be preparing for a weekly group meeting. In this meeting you will be an active participant because of your personal study. One lesson is to be completed each week, prior to coming to the weekly group meeting.

The weekly group meeting for this course features a discussion of the lesson that you have studied during the week. It also includes other elements to encourage group life, and to guide group members toward personal application of the material. The meeting, planned for at least a full hour, should be led by a person who enjoys leading discussions and helping people learn. The study leader will study the lesson in the same way as anyone else in the group. In addition, a **Leader's Guide** is available, with specific suggestions for conducting each weekly group meeting. This **Leader's Guide** can be obtained from:

David C. Cook Publishing Co.
850 North Grove Avenue
Elgin, IL 60120

or:

Lay Action Ministry Program, Inc.
7200 E. Dry Creek Road, Suite D-202
Englewood, CO 80112

PREPARING FOR BIBLE STUDY

A Personal Foundation for Effective Bible Study

Bible study resembles most things we do in life—the better we are prepared for it, the greater will be our reward. Our spiritual lives, as well as our Bible study experiences, will be greatly enhanced if we pray by faith that God will prepare us in a special way for Bible study. Pray for the "foundations" below:

Personal Foundations for Bible Study

1. A NEW HEART. Before personally receiving Christ, we were dead to real spiritual understanding because of our sins. Through Him we have been made alive, and a relationship with the Lord has been established (Eph. 2:1-10). One of the blessings of this new relationship is that we now have the capacity to understand the truths of Scripture (I Cor. 2:10-16).

The first foundation for Bible study is:

A new capacity to understand the truths of the Bible. Acquired through the new birth.

Be prepared to share your Christian experience during your next weekly group meeting. In the space below, tell how you came to a personal faith in Christ.

At fifteen I came under a growing conviction of personal sin. One Sunday I placed my complete reliance upon Christ + His death as my sin-bearing substitute. I was completely forgiven and God came into my life forever.

_____

_____

_____

_____

_____

_____

2. (A HUNGRY HEART.) Most new believers are blessed with a desire to know more about God's Word. While rebuking the Devil, Jesus said, "Man shall not live on bread alone, but on every word that proceeds out of the mouth of God" (Mt. 4:4). *Spiritual vitality depends on regular intake* *growth*

In Psalm 42:1 we read, "As the deer pants for [longs for] the water brooks, so my soul pants for Thee, O God." And I Peter 2:2 tells us that as newborn babes we are to "long for the pure milk of the word." A person who is truly spiritually hungry is not easily turned away, for the human soul needs food just as does the body. Is it not to this end that David urges, "O taste and see that the Lord is good" (Psalm 34:8)?

The second foundation for effective Bible study is

A desire for spiritual vitality + growth.

Through Bible study.

What evidences of a hungry heart can you think of?

Insistence, Persistence, Creativity,

Open + Honest, Personally demanding

What life-style activities encourage a hunger for spiritual things?

① Being with other Christians who are hungry to grow. ② The more we are serving the more we feel a need to be fed + grow to serve more effectively.

3. (AN OBEDIENT HEART.) Obedience to God is indispensable for effective Christian living. In John 14:15 Jesus says, "If you love Me, you will keep My command-

ments." And in verse 21 He adds, "He who has My commandments, and keeps them, he it is who loves Me." And again, in John 15:14, Jesus says, "You are My friends, if you do what I command you."

How is this truth about obeying God illustrated in James 1:22-25? *A man looks into a mirror and sees something important is missing or deficient.*

Doesn't give the matter due attention.

A Lack = absence or shortage.

But in spiritual matters it is not just something that should be desired, it is something that is required.

Disregard Ignore Explain it away Neglect Deny Overlook through haste or lack of carefulness Forget

T. Norton Sterrett says: "The Bible calls for response, not just analysis. If we are unwilling to act, we cannot reach the full truth. A disobedient heart means a closed understanding. An obedient heart finds the meaning of the Scripture opened." (The basic idea of this lesson was taken from Sterrett's, *How to Understand Your Bible*, © 1974 by Inter-Varsity Christian Fellowship of the USA and used by permission of InterVarsity Press, Downers Grove, IL 60515.)

What are some practical things you can do to increase your obedience to God's truth?

Increase your careful and respectful attention to it. / Issue is self-discipline. / Just do it / Pray that God will help you to do what you need to do. / ask for help / Be accountable to another. / Deal responsibly w/ temptations. / Don't Quit

Spirit is willing, flesh is weak. Take control of your flesh. 1 Cor 9:27

What commands do you find in Ephesians 4:22-24 and Galatians 5:16 relating to practical obedience?

Lay aside old choices dictated by corrupted lusts. Put on new choices that are holy + righteous.

Only accomplished through help + power of H.S.

The third foundation for effective Bible study is:

To respond to the truth.

4. A PERSISTENT HEART. Bible study will often be very thrilling as the Lord shows you some new truth or application of truth. At other times, however, such study may

13

be somewhat difficult and laborious. How we respond to these difficult times is crucial. Many people begin worthwhile tasks, but never complete them. Persistence in Bible study, as in life, is very important. Jesus' words in Matthew 7:7, 8 can help us here. We need to keep on asking, seeking, and knocking as we try to understand God's Word. Ask God for a persistent heart as you begin this study. It may be necessary at times to adjust the how or when of your study, but never give up and just walk away from it. The need for spiritual nourishment is just too great for that; the work of Christ through you must not be hindered.

The fourth foundation for Bible study is:

Don't quit. Persistent Persuit of Applied Truth.

What are some practical things you can do to develop greater persistence in Bible study?

Accountable/ Memorize the verses that tell us to study the Bible./ Think in light of eternity (will God say well-done) - what you can do to work toward that.

5. A TEACHABLE HEART. A teachable heart wants to go on learning. It never says, "I know enough." King David demonstrated a teachable spirit when he prayed, "Make me know Thy ways, O Lord; Teach me Thy paths. Lead me in Thy truth and teach me" (Ps. 25:4, 5; compare Ps. 86:11). In Psalm 32:8, 9 God says, "I will instruct you and teach you in the way which you should go; I will counsel you with My eye upon you. Do not be as the horse or as the mule which have no understanding."

A teachable heart is one of the most important qualities to pray for as you approach Bible study. Each time you come to read or study Scripture your prayer should be that of Psalm 119:18: "Open my eyes, that I may behold wonderful things from Thy law." How important it is to have a humble and teachable heart! If you

14

do, God will show you many wonderful things from His Word.

The fifth part of a personal foundation for effective Bible study is:

Be teachable

We have discussed five foundational requirements for effective Bible study. Reflect on them again: a new heart, a hungry heart, an obedient heart, a persistent heart, a teachable heart. Which of these attitudes would you like God to help you cultivate in your life?

Obedience + Persistence

The more we possess these attitudes, the more God will speak to us from His Word. We can have more of them just by asking . . . in simple faith. Ask God specifically about areas of need in your practice of Bible study, as well as for His special blessing on your participation in this course. _Let's pray now!_

Assumptions About Bible Study

Not inspiring but inspired

THE BIBLE IS GOD'S WORD. The Bible is uniquely inspired by God. Though many different human writers were involved—writing at different times in the history of Israel and the Christian Church—nevertheless, God was able to use each of these different individuals to write just what He wanted said.

Two verses are particularly clear about the divine inspiration of Scripture. Read both of them carefully. For your group meeting this week, memorize one of them. Write this verse on the back of a calling card and carry it with you for memorizing and reviewing.

All Scripture is inspired by God and profitable for teaching, for reproof, for correction, for training in righteousness (II Tim. 3:16).

For no prophecy was ever made by an act of human will, but men moved by the Holy Spirit spoke from God (II Pet. 1:21).

15

Our first assumption is: _____

The Bible is God's inerrant Word. [handwritten]
T/F — Powerful & Authoritative [handwritten]

THE HOLY SPIRIT IS OUR TEACHER. Let us praise God for
the word in John 16:13: "He [the Holy Spirit] will guide
you into all the truth" (John 16:13). Also, Jesus prom-
ised that the Father would send the Holy Spirit, who
"will teach you all things" (John 14:26; compare I John
2:20, 27). These are indeed precious promises from
God. As you come to the study of His Word, ask the
Holy Spirit to help you in your study.

This dependence on the Holy Spirit to teach us will
guard us against two wrong attitudes: placing too much
confidence in ourselves, and failing to trust the Lord for
needed understanding.

Of course, dependence on the Holy Spirit does not
mean that study is unnecessary. God may sometimes
quickly give us understanding of a particular passage,
while at other times we may have to study patiently for
insight.

Cults error [handwritten margin note]

Our second assumption, *We need the H.S.*
to guide our study. The H.S. will guide us. [handwritten]
will guard against the two dangers of *placing too*
much confidence in ourselves [handwritten]
and *failing to trust the Lord* [handwritten]
for needed understanding [handwritten].

TRANSLATIONS ARE CLEAR. The New Testament was orig-
inally written in the simple, everyday language of the
common people of the first century. Little attempt was
made to use the more difficult and less known classical
Greek of the educated people. God wanted His Word in
a form that could be clearly understood by the common
people, and this is still God's plan for the Bible today.

The very first translation of the Bible was of the Old
Testament, made for Greek-speaking Jews in the third

16

century before Christ. This translation, called the *Septuagint*, was frequently used by Christ and the apostles. It is still in print and read today.

Since the time of this first Bible translation, there have been many other translations, of both the Old and the New Testament. Some of the earliest of these translations were the Syriac, Coptic, and Old Latin. In keeping with the evident purpose of God that His Word be readily understandable in the language of the common people, hundreds of other language translations have since been made.

In recent years there has been a profusion of English language translations—leaving many people wondering how these different versions can all equally be the Word of God. The answer is that each translation is based upon the original languages to a greater or lesser degree of literalness. Translators are constantly faced with the difficult decision of whether to translate only the words, or *meanings* as well. For example, in Spanish there is a common expression which, if translated word for word, would be rendered in English as: "Don't pull my hair!" But if you were translating the phrase into English, wouldn't you say, "Don't pull my leg!"? You would probably try to translate the English *meaning* of the phrase. On the other hand, there are times when you would want the exact word for word translation. Bible translations can be categorized on the basis of whether they focus more on translating words, meanings, or a combination.

Dr. Donald Burdick, professor of New Testament at Denver Seminary, classifies translations in four categories:

1. Word-for-word translations. Two examples using this literal approach are the *American Standard Bible* and the *New American Standard Bible*.

2. Paraphrase translations. On the opposite end of this spectrum are translations following a free paraphrase of

meanings. While this method has the advantage of producing a very readable text, Burdick notes that "the further it moves from the wording of the original text the more danger there is of misinterpretation and inaccuracy." *The Living Bible* and Phillips's *New Testament in Modern English* are examples of this translation approach.

3. Equivalence translations. The equivalence method seeks to avoid both awkward literalness and unjustified interpretations. *The New English Bible, Beck,* and *Today's English Version* are cited as examples using this approach. *N I V*

4. Combination translations. A fourth approach seeks to retain the word-for-word literalness of the original languages, but shifts to an equivalence approach when necessary to translate Hebrew and Greek idioms into our own culture (as in the Spanish example above).

For serious Bible study, you should use a fairly literal translation (such as the *New American Standard Bible,* used in this course) since a paraphrase does add interpretive words and expressions.

The availability of so many English versions does not mean that the study of Greek and Hebrew is unimportant. Such study, especially with the aid of the many Bible study tools available for Greek and Hebrew students, can be exceedingly helpful. But since most Christians do not know these languages, they can rejoice in the quality English translations available, knowing that God's truth can be adequately understood in them.

Our third assumption is:

The Modern (more literal) Translations clarify the Word for us.

How does the common Greek language of the original New Testament writings support the statement that God intends His Word to be clearly understood?

It was written in the Common language of the ordinary people, not the classical Greek

WE CAN GAIN ADEQUATE, BUT NOT PERFECT UNDERSTAND-
ING. We confess that we are but mortals; therefore, our
capacity for understanding God's Word is sometimes
less than adequate. Even with the best of understanding (including knowledge of the original languages), it
will not be possible to understand perfectly all the
truths of Scripture. Even the apostle Peter confessed
that in Paul's writings there were "some things hard to
understand" (II Pet. 3:16). Many subsequent Bible students have been forced to agree! For example, what
does Paul mean when he speaks about some who were
"baptized for the dead" (I Cor. 15:29)? Or Peter, when
he talks about Christ preaching to the spirits in prison
(I Pet. 3:19)? These, and other difficult passages, keep
us humble as we realize that, in this life, we will never
understand everything perfectly.

But don't worry. There is more than enough that we
can understand to show us clearly the way to life and
the way to live. Someone has said that what troubled
him was not the passages of Scripture that he *didn't*
understand, but those that he *did*! The great need is to
live in the light—that is, to obey those passages we do
understand.

Our fourth assumption is that: We can understand
everything we need to.

SCRIPTURE INTERPRETS SCRIPTURE. The Bible serves as its
own best interpreter. Careful study of the clearer passages of Scripture often sheds light on the more per-
plexing passages. Here are some ways to apply this
principle:

1. Discover the author's purpose for writing. At times
this will be critical to a correct interpretation.

2. Carefully examine the context. The immediate context includes the verses (and sometimes paragraphs)
found before and after the verse under study. Many
erroneous interpretations of Scripture, leading to seri-

ous doctrinal errors, have been the result of failure to observe the true context of a passage.

3. Use cross-references. By finding verses that speak to the same subject, you can get a fuller understanding of the passage under study. (This approach, however, can be abused. Sometimes the cross-reference verse only superficially alludes to the same truth, and is not truly helpful.)

Be careful here.

4. Use the New Testament to interpret the Old Testament. Remember that New Testament Scripture is a fulfillment of the Old Testament. The way Jesus and the apostles interpreted the Old Testament is a reliable guide to how we should interpret it as well.

Our fifth assumption is: *Be honest & careful + let the Scriptures speak.*

GATHERING THE TOOLS FOR BIBLE STUDY

Craftsmen, such as carpenters, plumbers, and mechanics, can only work effectively when they have the proper tools for their trade. This is true of dentists, doctors, and lawyers as well. As a student of the Bible, you, too, will need some basic tools in order to enjoy success as a student of Scripture.

In this lesson you will examine several important reference books. These are your Bible study "tools," and you will need to have regular access to them. Try to purchase them for your own personal library. These books will be exceedingly helpful to you throughout a lifetime of meaningful Bible study.

A Study Bible

A good study Bible is the most important Bible study tool that you will ever purchase. Here are some tips in selecting one:

LOOK FOR A BIBLE WITH GOOD CROSS-REFERENCES AND MARGINAL READINGS. Some Bibles also contain a concordance (a list of important words used in the Bible, with accompanying references). This can often be helpful in looking for cross-references, but for most verse hunting you will need a more complete concordance.

LOOK FOR A BIBLE WITHOUT A LOT OF INTERPRETIVE NOTES. Your purpose in using a study Bible is to study the

Scriptures for yourself, without notes that lead you along the lines of someone else's thinking.

FIND A BIBLE WITH WIDE MARGINS. Use the margins for your own personal study notes. (Make sure the paper is thick enough for writing.) Your carefully written notes can prove very helpful to you later on.

MAKE SURE THE BIBLE HAS A GOOD SET OF MAPS, WITH AN ACCOMPANYING INDEX. Some Bible maps are so imprecise or difficult to read that they are of little value.

LAMP does not "recommend" one Bible translation or edition over another. The *New King James Bible* may be an ideal choice for some. For a Bible with excellent cross-references and additional margin space, it is hard to beat a study edition of the *New American Standard Bible*. The *Thompson Chain Reference Bible* contains a tremendous amount of study helps and is now available in either the KJV or the NIV. Many other good study Bibles are also available. Your pastor may have specific recommendations which will be helpful to you.

Of the suggestions made for selecting a study Bible, the first three are the most important. They are:

_____

_____

_____

A Notebook

What you write down as you study your Bible—your thoughts, observations, and other notes—these are of great value to you. Not that they are all "gems" you will cherish forever. But they are valuable because they have stimulated your thought processes. When you come back to them in the future, they may lead you into new avenues of study to pursue, or give you ideas for developing good group discussion questions.

Although a notebook for this course is not essential, you will want one for your future Bible studies. We suggest that it be of convenient size, and loose leaf. Its capacity for adding and rearranging pages will prove very helpful. The 8½-by-5½-inch, three-ring notebook is a practical size to accompany your study Bible and is readily available in stationery stores.

Bible Marking Pencils

You can use a few colored pencils to highlight aspects of the truth you are studying. For example, use yellow to highlight promises, and orange to note warnings in Scripture. Green can suggest growth; blue for commands of God. Other colors can be used according to the particular system you choose. Whatever colors you use, follow a consistent system. That is, if orange is used to note warnings in Scripture, this color should *always* indicate warnings. (Caution: colored markers can bleed through the paper; colored pencils will not.)

Another helpful tool is a thin-line (0.5 or 0.7) mechanical pencil, with colored or regular lead. With it you can carefully write in your own markings, notes, and brief comments. Colored lead will not smudge, yet can be erased. Regular ball-point pens cannot be erased and sometimes later bleed through thin Bible paper.

A Concordance

A good concordance is a very basic and important tool for Bible study, but not essential to complete this course. The one you may already have in the back of your study Bible is sometimes helpful, but not adequate for most purposes. You can use a concordance for a number of Bible study functions:

1. As a "verse finder." You might, for example, remember a passage, or just a part of a passage, and want to locate it in your Bible. To do this, take a key word from the passage (preferably, the least common word—one that is unlikely to be found in a number of different passages) and look it up in the alphabetically arranged concordance. You will find a list of all the verses where this word is found.

2. For cross-reference study. Concordances contain much more cross-reference material than does the best study Bible. The procedure here is to select a word from the passage under study, and locate its *other* occurrences in the Scriptures. Much additional material can often be found in this way. Beginning Bible students need to be careful not to take cross-reference verses out of context when using this method.

3. To study topics and biographies. To use this method, select the topic word, perhaps including related words, and study each of them as they occur in the Bible. Then organize this material, selecting important passages for a topical study.

4. As a dictionary. *→ Strongs* Concordances containing the original Hebrew and Greek words give brief definitions, and also help you distinguish between two or more of the original language words that may be translated by only one English word.

Many different concordances are available today. The two major differences in concordances are: the degree of completeness, and the translation on which they are based.

Crudens has been a household word in Christian homes for over 200 years. It is presently in print in several editions. If you decide to purchase a *Cruden's Concordance*, be sure to buy the "complete" edition. Some editions are less than complete, and, therefore, less useful. It is better to spend a little more and get the edition that will be much more useful in your study. *Cruden's* is based on the King James Version.

Strong's Exhaustive Concordance and *Young's Analytical Concordance* are both more complete concordances based on the King James Version. These large volumes are indeed exhaustive (and not just because of their

24

sheer bulk and weight!) because they note every occurrence of every word in Scripture. They also list the Hebrew and Greek words, and give their meanings. *Strong's* lists these meanings in a section at the end of the volume, and *Young's* at the beginning of each new word listing. Either is recommended for students most familar with the King James Version.

Other concordances are based on modern translations rather than on the King James Version. If you are more familiar with a modern version of the Bible, you may want a concordance based on that version. For the NASB there is the *New American Standard Exhaustive Concordance*, for the RSV there is *Nelson's Complete Concordance*, and for the NIV there is the *NIV Complete Concordance*. The *Zondervan Expanded Concordance* has additional word listings for several modern translations. The *New American Standard Exhaustive Concordance* is particularly recommended.

The two major differences in concordances are:

Degree of completeness.
Translation it is based on.

Why may the modern language concordances be of particular value to some students?

Because they are more familiar with modern translations

A Bible Dictionary

A good Bible dictionary contains important information on almost every topic mentioned in the Bible: studies on Bible books, historical and cultural background, studies of doctrinal subjects, and archaeological findings.

There are several good Bible dictionaries in print, including *The New Bible Dictionary* (Eerdmans); *Pictorial*

Bible Dictionary (Zondervan); *Unger's Bible Dictionary* (Moody); and *Davis Dictionary of the Bible* (Baker). Multi-volume Bible encyclopedias serve the same purpose in more depth, but they are much more expensive and expansive!

Why is a good Bible dictionary an important tool for Bible study?

You can learn important background + explanatory information that enables you to better understand the Scripture.

A Bible Atlas

The Bible atlas helps you locate places named in the Bible. Your study of almost any portion of Scripture will be enhanced as you examine the place or places in their geographical setting. How helpful it is, for example, to see God's leadership in the conquest of Canaan: Joshua first divides the area into two parts, then sweeps to victory in the south, following with campaigns in the north. Or, in the New Testament, you can use your atlas to carefully observe the missionary movements of the apostle Paul as he carried God's Good News to the Gentiles. Locating places in a Bible atlas also affords an opportunity to note other relevant geographical features, such as distances involved in travel, and the terrain of the region. This helps you visualize where Bible events took place, making Bible study more meaningful and interesting.

What should you look for in a Bible atlas? The following guidelines may prove helpful.

- Maps should be clear and bright.
- Many names should appear on them in clear print.
- A gazetteer should accompany the maps, providing a code to guide in locating Bible names on them.

- There should be a number of maps, covering each major era of Bible history.
- Clear indications of elevations and rainfall are also valuable.

One of the best, reasonably priced atlases is *Hammond's Atlas of the Bible Lands*. The *Compact Bible Atlas with Gazetteer*, published by Baker, is also very good. The primary value of a Bible atlas is:

Location of places in the Bible to see them in their geographical setting and distances & terrain

Bible Commentaries

Commentaries are just what the name implies: they comment on a Bible passage to explain, illustrate, or even apply its meaning. Commentaries are not a cure-all for all problems of understanding the text. For example, you may turn to a particular commentary and find that it does not say anything at all about the passage you need clarified. This is particularly a problem with the one-volume commentaries covering the entire Bible. But it may also occur in commentaries that cover a single book. Then, too, coming as it does from the pen of mere humans, the commentary may not always be entirely correct. They do not always agree with each other (and they can't all be right!). Nevertheless, most commentaries were written by mature, godly persons, and we should read them carefully, with due respect.

The main differences in commentaries are: some are one volume, others multivolume, and still others cover only one Bible book. While some are exegetical (that is, dealing with the meaning of the text), others are more devotional, dealing with the application of Bible truth. While many have been written by evangelical scholars, some have been written by scholars not holding to a high view of the inspiration of Scripture.

Before buying any commentary, check with your pastor. He will doubtless have some excellent suggestions.

In the multivolume sets, the Tyndale series of commentaries provides a wealth of helpful information. For more complete coverage, the New International Commentary series, or the Expositors Bible Commentary series are excellent choices. Many good single-book commentaries are also available. David C. Cook offers the Basic Bible Series, which provides general comment on Scripture portions, for individual or group study. Two main differences in commentaries are:

Exegetical

Devotional

Should you decide to buy just one commentary on Ephesians for this course, we suggest either the Tyndale series on Ephesians, or John R. W. Stott's God's New Society. You will need to consult a commentary on Ephesians throughout your study in this course.

Time out! Have you been able to obtain your own copy of the Bible study tools covered in this lesson? What are these tools again?

1. A good study Bible
2. Bible-marking pencils (and a notebook for later study)
3. Concordance
4. Bible dictionary
5. Bible atlas
6. Bible commentary

• New Treasury of Scripture Knowledge

• Topical Bible

Every serious student of Scripture should purchase each of these tools as soon as possible. They should be regarded as indispensable basics for your study and preparation to minister to others. The tools listed above (except the concordance) are necessary to complete this course.

Where can you obtain these items? Visit your local Christian bookstore. Probably all of these tools will be available there. You should examine the various titles available before making your purchase.

Or, write directly to LAMP. In the event a Bible book store is not near you, these books may be ordered by mail. If you are not able to purchase books right away, use one of the following options as a stop-gap, in order to successfully complete this course: 1) Consult your church library. Some of these volumes may be available to check out. 2) Check with your pastor or other people you know who might have some of these books. Perhaps they would be willing to lend them.

DISCOVERING THE AUTHOR'S PURPOSE

Have you ever listened to a public speaker and been unable to grasp his point? If you are like me, you became frustrated and even a little exasperated. Your mind shouts out, "What's he driving at?" or, "If she would just clearly say what she means!"

In order to understand what Scripture is teaching, you must first discover the author's purpose for writing a particular Bible book. This will help you see the original context, and indicate the direction and theme of the book's message.

Approaches to Finding the Author's Purpose

Occasionally the writer of a Bible book clearly states his purpose for writing. The apostle John does this, both in his gospel, and in his first epistle. Study the following Scripture passages. What is the author's stated purpose in each case?

John 20:31 _Evangelistic_

I John 5:13 _Assurance_

Luke 1:1-3 _Tell the story of Christ so others will believe._

More often, however, the author's purpose is not clearly stated, but may be implied from certain statements he makes. Paul's first letter to the Corinthians is an example of this. Read I Corinthians 1:11, 7:1. What provided the "agenda" for this letter, thus determining Paul's purpose?

*Problems in the church reported*
*to Paul*

Notice how this agenda is alluded to in 5:1, 8:1, 12:1, and 16:1. From this information you can easily develop an outline of the book, consistent with Paul's purpose.

Most of the time, however, the best way to discover the author's purpose is to carefully read the text—looking for the major idea or ideas developed by the Biblical writer. What do you see as Paul's major purpose for writing the Book of Galatians, based on Galatians 1:6-9; 3:1-5; and 5:1-6?

_____

_____

_____

Three ways to discover the author's purpose are:

*Author clearly states purpose*

*Implied*

*Carefully read the text looking*
*for major idea(s) developed*

Steps to Discovering the Author's Purpose in Ephesians

Now let's put into practice what you have learned so far, by trying to discover the author's purpose and plan in the Book of Ephesians. To complete this assignment you will probably need to spend longer than the usual one hour. But reading and rereading Scripture for better understanding will be some of your best-spent time.

Whoops! It's a "no-no" to look at any other source except the text of the Bible for this study. An outstanding Bible teacher, James M. Gray, maintained that one's own independent study of Scripture, as imperfect as it might be, is of far more practical value than the most perfect outline prepared by someone else.

Jot down what you find as you complete the following steps:

STEP ONE. Skim quickly through the Book of Ephesians, looking for obvious indications of the author's purpose. Write anything you notice in the space below.

> 1:10; 2:11 — a plan to unite all things in Christ
> 1:15 Paul had heard of Ephesians faith + wanted to strengthen them in it. (see 4-6
> 3:1, 13 Paul refers to his prison circumstances

STEP TWO. Now read Ephesians much more carefully. Look at each of the subjects covered. Write down several of the important ideas or topics as you see Paul presenting them. Look for evidences of purpose from your list of specific subjects dealt with in the epistle.

> 1:3-23 Paul's Prayer
> 2:1-10 Believer's life b/f + after conversion

2:11-3:20 Relationship of Gentiles
    to Jews in Body of Christ
4:1-16 Body growing through
    exercise of Spiritual Gifts
4:17-5:21 Practical applications
    of Christs filling believer
5:21-6:9 Submission
6:10-19 Believers armor

STEP THREE. Combine the information gathered in steps
one and two, and state what appears to you to be the
author's overall purpose (or purposes) in writing.

Preparing the Believer
    to Impact his world.

Finding the author's purpose is both very important,
as well as very rewarding. It is an approach that can be
used with any book of the Bible.

4

DISCOVERING THE AUTHOR'S PLAN

Dr. Nelaton, the great French surgeon, once said that if he had four minutes to perform a lifesaving operation, he would take at least one minute to consider how best to do it. In surgery, as with any endeavor of life, prior planning helps assure the intended outcome.

But what about the Bible? Did the authors of the Bible also have a plan as they wrote their books? Yes! Through the special guidance of the Holy Spirit, the Bible has come about, not as a hodgepodge of disjointed writings, but as an orderly whole. And within each Bible book itself, one can discern a logical order and purpose in thematic development. In fact, interpreting Bible passages begins with discovering this inner framework of the entire Bible book.

In this lesson your goal is to divide the Book of Ephesians into segments of appropriate length for group Bible studies. Build on what you learned in Lesson 3 about the overall theme and major topics from Ephesians.

Develop an Outline

Let's begin by illustrating this approach from I Corinthians. It seems clear that Paul based the first part of his letter on information received about problems in the church (see I Cor. 1:11). Segments which would be appropriate for individual studies in I Corinthians are:

35

- A problem of divisions in the church, 1:10-31
- Paul's example regarding this problem, 2:1-16
- A problem of church carnality, 3:1-23
- A problem of spiritual pride, 4:1-21
- A problem regarding immorality, 5:1-13
- A problem regarding lawsuits, 6:1-11
- The immorality problem continued, 6:12-20

Paul then states in 7:1, "Now concerning the things about which you wrote." In the second half of I Corinthians Paul responds to matters brought to his attention in their letter. Segments appropriate in length for individual Bible studies are:

- The question of marriage, 7:1-40
- The Christian response to food offered to idols (discussed in chap. 8; illustrated in 9:1—10:22; and concluded in 10:23-33)
- Spiritual gifts for the Church, chapter 12
- Spiritual gifts versus love, chapter 13
- The practice of tongues versus prophecy, chapter 14
- Teaching about the Resurrection, chapter 15

Now it's your turn. Read through the Book of Ephesians once again. In the space below, write down in greater detail the main ideas you find. Note where topics begin and end, and how these topics relate to the overall theme. Try to let one segment (i.e., a Bible study) focus on one primary topic. Keep in mind that paragraph divisions often aid in seeing the larger picture in the book.

Passage / Main Idea

_____

_____

_____

_____

_____

_____

_____

_____

_____

_____

_____

_____

_____

_____

_____

_____

_____

_____

_____

_____

_____

_____

_____

Make Adjustments

The work you have just completed should "fit in" with what you learned in Lesson 3 about finding the author's purpose. To put this another way, your outline of the book should be a development, or expansion, of this purpose. Each part of the outline should cover a particular aspect of the author's overall purpose so that all the points of the outline will add up to a concise summary of the content. Does your outline do this?

Look back to page 34 to see your first statement of the author's purpose. Write it again here.

_____

_____

_____

At this point you may want to change parts of your outline to better fit your statement of purpose. On the other hand, if you feel that your outline reflects the content of Ephesians quite well, you may want to adjust the wording of your statement of purpose to better fit your outline. Make any improvement you can in the space below.

Purpose _____

_____

_____

Passage / Main Idea

_____

_____

_____

_____

_____

_____

_____

_____

_____

_____

_____

_____

5

EXAMINING THE HISTORICAL BACKGROUND

Before traveling to a foreign country many tourists have found it helpful to study the culture and values of the people they are going to visit. This makes for a more meaningful and enjoyable visit—both for them and for the host people.

Something of this same situation exists as we come to the study of Scripture. Here we are walking into a culture that existed over 2,000 years ago! Obviously, if we are to understand and apply God's Word correctly, we must understand the historical setting in which it was written.

Kinds of Background Information

The events of the Bible took place at particular points in history, in specific places, and within various cultural situations. The study of these will help us better understand, appreciate, and even interpret a book or passage of Scripture. Let's look at this by way of a few illustrations:

HISTORICAL BACKGROUND. Daniel was made the "third ruler" in the kingdom of Babylon (Dan. 5:16) because of the ability God had given him to interpret the king's dreams. Many readers of Scripture have asked, Who then was the "second ruler," in rank between Daniel and the king? From a study of *history* we learn that this person was doubtless Belshazzar himself because his father Nabonidus was still alive and technically the first ruler in the kingdom.

GEOGRAPHICAL BACKGROUND. In John 4:4, Jesus "had to pass through Samaria." Why? Was it because He knew the woman of Samaria was there and that she needed His ministry? Doubtless this was an important reason. But by looking at a map of the area we see another factor: Samaria was *geographically located* between Judea and Galilee.

CULTURAL BACKGROUND. The request of one of Jesus' disciples to "permit me first to go and bury my father" (Matthew 8:21) before forsaking all to follow Jesus, may seem reasonable enough—until one learns that this was a *cultural* expression meaning "Let me care for my father until he passes away."

List three types of background information which you should look for in Bible study.

Historical

Geographical

Cultural

When to Look for Background Information

Looking for relevant background information should not be the first step in your study of a book or passage of Scripture. As indicated in the previous lessons, you should first observe the text itself—read and carefully glean from it all that you possibly can, making notes of your observations.

After completing this initial study, however, you should spend some time looking elsewhere for additional background information. The right time to look for background information is:

After you have observed the text itself.

Where to Look for Background Information

The first place to look is in the *cross-references* of your study Bible. Frequently the New Testament refers to things that occurred in the Old. Knowing this information can significantly help you understand the New Testament passage under study. Or, the New Testament may in turn help explain or apply the truth of the Old Testament.

For example, suppose you are studying John chapter 3. In verse 14 you read: "As Moses lifted up the serpent in the wilderness." Now what, you ask yourself, does this refer to? The New American Standard study Bible lists Numbers 21:9 as a cross-reference. From this verse you learn that Moses had made a bronze image of a serpent and set it on a pole. Those bitten by "fiery serpents" could look at it and be healed.

Let's take another example, this one from the passage you will be studying later in this course. Turn to Ephesians 1:1 in your study Bible. Look for a small letter immediately before the word "Ephesus." Does this give a cross-reference to Acts 18:19? If not, look for it on page 54 of this book. In Acts 18:19 the word "Ephesus" also gives a number of cross-references where this word occurs in other places in the New Testament, including Acts 19. The Acts chapter records many events from Paul's ministry in Ephesus. Read Acts 19 now. List the main points that are relevant to Paul's mission and the establishment of a Christian work in that city.

Disciples of John the B.

and saved

There was a synagogue (10 or more Jews)

30

Taught 2 yrs in School of Tyrannus.

Ephesus 50

Both Jews & Greeks heard Word

Ephesians 60

Paul did miracles

7 Jewish Exorcists refuted / All sec.

Burned magic books

Idol makers revolt.

Ephesus is "guardian of Temple of Great Artemis"

43

_____

_____

_____

_____

The first place you should look for information on the historical background is:

_____Cross-References_____

The second place to look for background information is the geographical references on the maps in your *Bible atlas*. For example, by reading the Book of Joshua together with a period map of the land of Palestine, you can increase your appreciation of how God led Joshua to a brilliant military conquest of Caanan. Similarly, locating the "cities of refuge" (Joshua 20) will reveal the wise strategic placement of each of them.

Using a Bible map, locate the province of Asia. Fill in the area with a colored pencil. Write in the name of this province, and color the area it covers. Now look at the size of this province, using the scale of miles chart provided in the map. It is approximately _500 300_ miles North to South, and _650_ miles East to West.

44

Background information can also be obtained from:

Bible Atlas

The third place to look for background information is your *Bible dictionary*. For example, in a study of the Book of Ephesians you would read the article on "Ephesus" in your Bible dictionary. Read this article now. Note in the space below the things you learned about its geographical importance, its religions, and other features that add to what you learned from Acts 19.

Ephsus — Capital of Asia
Opulant City
Diana Temple 7 Wonders
Timothy pastored
Serious Riot

How can the information you just wrote be useful to you as you lead Bible studies?

6

HEAD:
STUDYING BIBLE PORTIONS

You are now ready to learn about the HEAD, HEART, and HANDS approach to Bible study, to be covered in Lessons 6 through 10.

HEAD. Your first concern should be to develop a correct and adequate *understanding* of what the passage says. This course will help you carefully observe what the text says, and guide you in learning what it means. (The HEAD aspect of Bible study will be covered in this lesson, and in Lessons 7 and 8.)

HEART. Your second concern is the *application of truth to your own life.* Like a good cook, you want not only to prepare the meal, but to enjoy it as well. Each of your study periods should include a time when you let the Word speak to your own heart and guide your life. (The HEART aspect of Bible study will be covered in Lesson 9.)

HANDS. Finally, you should be willing to *share with others what you learn.* This course will help you prepare to teach these lessons in a discussion-type Bible study of Ephesians. This kind of study group can meet in a home, an office, or a Sunday school class. It can be done with friends and neighbors, or just with your own family. If you are planning to teach the Book of Ephesians to others, you will need to set aside at least one additional hour each week for personal study and preparation. (The HANDS aspect of Bible study will be unfolded in Lesson 10.)

Describe the HEAD, HEART, and HANDS approach to Bible study:

Head — getting a good understanding of what the text says + what it means. Heart — applying it to me. Hands — teaching it to others.

Know (of)
affect
Do

The HEAD approach to Bible study is based upon the following five steps. Following these steps every time you study a Bible portion will help you understand both what the passage *says*, and what it *means*:

One: Read Prayerfully

Keep an open mind to receive God's message for you. The Bible is a spiritual book and can only be understood with the aid of the Spirit (I Cor. 2:10). Each time we come to study the Bible our prayer should be along the lines of Psalm 119:18: "Open my eyes, that I may behold wonderful things from Thy law."

Two: Read Repeatedly and Thoughtfully

Time spent just reading the text—reading and reading it again, can be the most worthwhile time you spend in study. One well-known Bible teacher reads a Bible book as much as 50 times before he feels ready to teach it. You may not be able to read it that many times, but the more you read it the more fruitful will be your study.

Three: Mark and Notate the Text

You can make various marks (such as underlining, arrows, asterisks, and any number of brief comments) to help you highlight portions of the text. The important thing is to make sure these symbols actually help you observe the text with a more discerning eye—rather than confuse or distract you. (As suggested in

48

Lesson 2, a fine-line mechanical pencil helps you do this neatly.)

Other Bible markings can be done with colored pencils, either by highlighting words (with lighter colors, such as yellow and orange), or by underlining or circling. A consistent color code is important. For example, if yellow is chosen to emphasize God's promises, it should have this meaning throughout your study Bible.

Four: Record Your Observations

The "observations" section on page 55, and in subsequent lessons, is designed for your personal notes, questions, and markings. What to look for and record:

1. ILLUSTRATIONS AND COMPARISONS. Such illustrations often bring out the author's meaning. An example of this is James 3:6-12, where the tongue is compared to a fire.

2. CONTRASTED IDEAS. The connective "but" often introduces a contrast. See Galatians 5:16-24.

3. REPEATED IDEAS. Repetition is used for emphasis in Scripture. For examples, see I Corinthians 13; Matthew 5:21-48; and James 2:14-26.

4. CAUSE-AND-EFFECT RELATIONSHIPS. The Old Testament prophets, for example, frequently spoke a warning, then told of what would happen if the warning went unheeded. Key words such as: because, for, in order that, therefore, and if, usually indicate cause and effect relationships.

What cause-and-effect relationship do you see in:

I John 1:5-7? *Having fellowship w/ one another + God results from walking in the light.*

James 3:13-18? *The tongue must be under control of Heavenly wisdom in order for life to be a blessing.*

5. GENERALIZATIONS AND SUMMARIES. Such statements may come either at the beginning or at the close of a discussion. Paul frequently makes a general assertive statement, then develops it in detail.

49 *Rom 12:1, 2 ff*
Eph 5:18 ff.

6. PROGRESSION OF THOUGHT AND ARRANGEMENT OF MATERI-
AL. Note this progression, for example, in Hebrews 11. *12:1,2*

7. THE AUTHOR'S QUESTIONS. Usually these questions either
(1) introduce a problem, or (2) provide a summary.
(They are often rhetorical questions, with the answer
being implied from the context.) Which of these two
purposes do you find in:

Romans 6:1-4 _summary_

James 3:13-18 _problem_

8. GRAMMATICAL CONSTRUCTIONS. Though some people
are turned off by this subject, it is helpful to note the
subject of the sentence, the action words, and the ob-
jects of the action. The tense of the action words (verbs)
is frequently very important. Adjectives and adverbs
describe other words, as do the longer phrases and
clauses. The author's choice of prepositions, such as:
in, through, with, by, to, and of, often significantly
influence the meaning. This is also true of connectives,
such as: because, therefore, yet, however, and likewise.

Eight kinds of observations that will help you understand the meaning of the text are:

1. _Illustrations + comparisons_
2. _Contrasted Ideas_
3. _Repeated Ideas_
4. _Cause + Effect relationships_
5. _Generalizations + summaries_
6. _Progression of Thought + arrangement_
7. _The author's Questions of material_
8. _Grammatical constructions_

Five: Ask the Text Questions

Asking questions will sharpen your understanding of
the text. In her book, *The Joy of Discovery* (Augsberg

50

Publishing House, © 1956, 1975. Used by permission). Oletta Wald has prepared the following helpful list of questions for probing deeper into the meaning of the text:

1. MEANING QUESTIONS: What is the meaning of this word, phrase, or statement? How can this word be defined? Is there a deeper meaning in the idea than appears on the surface? *Use dictionary + Thesaurus*

2. SIGNIFICANCE QUESTIONS: What is the significance of a key word, phrase, or statement in the passage? What is its importance to the message? What is the significance of the verb tenses, connectives, grammatical constructions? What is the significance of the literary patterns, such as comparisons, contrasts, illustrations, repetitions, structure of the passage? Why has the author used this particular term? Would it make any difference if this idea were left out? Or stated differently?

3. IMPLICATION QUESTIONS: What is implied by the use of this term or phrase? What is implied by the use of a question, an illustration, etc.?

4. RELATIONSHIP QUESTIONS: What is the relationship of words to other words? One part of a verse to another part? Verses to verses? Paragraphs with paragraphs? Chapters with chapters? Relationship of the beginning and end of a chapter or section?

5. PROGRESSION QUESTIONS: Is there any progression in the thought pattern? Does it move toward a climax? Is one idea built upon another? Is there any significance in the order of a series of words or ideas?

6. LITERAL OR FIGURATIVE QUESTIONS: Is this term or statement to be considered literally or figuratively?
   Author's intent.
   H.S. intent.

7

HEAD:
OBSERVING BIBLE PORTIONS

The best way to learn something is to *do* it! In your lesson this week you will carefully study Ephesians 1:1-14. Follow the sequence of steps discussed in the previous chapter (summarized below).

Remember the Steps!

1. Pray for God's blessing before you begin, and during your reading.

2. Read these verses repeatedly, and thoughtfully.

3. Make your own markings in the text—underlinings, arrows, brief comments—anything that is helpful to your understanding of the message of these verses.

4. Go through the list of observation suggestions (pp. 49 and 50) and record relevant comments on your observations page.

5. Ask the text questions—matters that you do not yet understand, or questions that serve to identify key issues or points crucial to understanding or applying the text. Record these on page 55.

Remember, this part of your study should be your own work. Don't look (at this stage) at any other source. Allow yourself a full hour or more.

Ephesians 1:1-14

PAUL, [a]an apostle of [b]Christ Jesus [1c]by the will of God, to the [2d]saints who are [3]at [e]Ephesus, and [f]*who are* faithful in [b]Christ Jesus:

2 [a]Grace to you and peace from God our Father and the Lord Jesus Christ.

3 [a]Blessed *be* the God and Father of our Lord Jesus Christ, who has blessed us with every spiritual blessing in [b]the heavenly *places* in Christ,

4 just as [a]He chose us in Him before [b]the foundation of the world, that we should be [c]holy and blameless before [1]Him. [d]In love

5 [1]He [a]predestined us to [b]adoption as sons through Jesus Christ to Himself, [c]according to the [2]kind intention of His will,

6 [a]to the praise of the glory of His grace, which He freely bestowed on us in [b]the Beloved.

7 [a]In [1]Him we have [b]redemption [c]through His blood, the [d]forgiveness of our trepasses, according to [e]the riches of His grace,

8 which He [1]lavished upon [2]us. In all wisdom and insight

9 He [1a]made known to us the mystery of His will, [b]according to His [2]kind intention which He [c]purposed in Him

10 with a view to an administration [1]suitable to [a]the fulness of the times, *that is,* [b]the summing up of all things in Christ, things [2]in the heavens and things upon the earth. In Him

11 [1]also we [2a]have obtained an inheritance, having been [b]predestined [c]according to His purpose who works all things [d]after the counsel of His will,

12 to the end that we who were the first to hope in [1]Christ should be [a]to the praise of His glory.

13 In [1]Him, you also, after listening to [a]the message of truth, the gospel of your salvation—having also [2]believed, you were [b]sealed in [1]Him with [c]the Holy Spirit of promise,

14 who is [1a]given as a pledge of [b]our inheritance, with a view to the [c]redemption of [d]*God's own* possession, [e]to the praise of His glory.

1 [1]Lit., *through* [2]I.e., true believers; lit., *holy ones* [3]Some ancient mss. omit, *at Ephesus* [a]2 Cor. 1:1 [b]Eph. 2:6, 7, 10, 13, 20; 3:1, 6, 11, 21; Col. 1:4; 2:6; 4:12; Rom. 8:1; Gal. 3:26 [c]1 Cor. 1:1 [d]Acts 9:13; Phil. 1:1; Col. 1:1 [c]Acts 18:19 [f]Col. 1:2

2 [a]Rom. 1:7

3 [a]2 Cor. 1:3 [b]Eph. 1:20; 2:6; 3:10; 6:12; Phil. 3:20

4 [1]Or, *Him, in love* [a]2 Thess. 2:13f.; Eph. 2:10 [b]Matt. 25:34 [c]Eph. 5:27; Col. 1:22; 2 Tim. 1:9 [d]Eph. 4:2, 15, 16; 5:2

5 [1]Lit., *having predestined* [2]Lit., *good pleasure* [a]Eph. 1:11; Rom. 8:29f.; Acts 13:48 [b]Rom. 8:14ff.; Gal. 4:5 [c]Luke 12:32; 1 Cor. 1:21; Gal. 1:15; Phil. 2:13; Col. 1:19

6 [a]Eph. 1:12, 14 [b]Matt. 3:17

7 [1]Lit., *whom* [a]Col. 1:14 [b]Eph. 1:14; 1 Cor. 1:30; Rom. 3:24 [c]Acts 20:28; Rom. 3:25 [d]Acts 2:38 [c]Rom. 2:4; Eph. 1:18; 2:7; 3:8, 16; Col. 1:27

8 [1]Lit., *made abundant toward* [2]Or, *us, in all wisdom and insight*

9 [1]Lit., *making known* [2]Lit., *good pleasure* [a]Rom. 11:25; 16:25; Eph. 3:3 [b]Luke 12:32; 1 Cor. 1:21; Gal. 1:15; Phil. 2:13; Col. 1:19 [c]Eph. 1:11; Rom. 8:28

v. 3 God is the cause or source
of all these blessings.

Observations   Personal Pronouns get
confusing.
1. Listing of 8 blessings for the believer.
2. Repitition of "in Christ" idea 13 X
            channel, Source
                        (cause + effect)
3. Verse 6 reflects either result or purpose.
                        (cause + effect)
4. V. 12 reflects purpose
                        (cause + effect)
5. v. 14 reflects either result or purpose.
6. v. 3 seems to be a summary statement
            which is illustrated + developed in
            4 - 14.
7. Divisions @ 3-6; 7-12; 13-14

        What are spiritual blessings? Cross-Ref.
                                Concord.

Verse/Questions How should we understand
"in heavenlies in Christ"? Define.
What is meant by "adoption" v. 5?
Paul seems to repetedly emphasize
God kindness + His sovereign
purpose to bless us. Is this
important? Is there any order
or progression of thought.

    What does v 10 mean?

55

_____

_____

_____

_____

_____

_____

_____

_____

_____

_____

_____

_____

_____

_____

_____

_____

For Next Class Hour

1. Be prepared to share with the group the particular system of symbol and color-code markings that you have adopted. Share examples of how you used them in this lesson.

2. Be prepared to share the observations you noted as you read and reread the text.

3. Be prepared to share the questions you asked the text. Your questions can also contribute to the learning experience of others in the group.

8

2ⁿᵈ Phase

HEAD:
UNDERSTANDING BIBLE PORTIONS

Martin Luther said, "I study my Bible as I gather apples. First, I shake the whole tree that the ripest might fall. Then I shake each limb, and when I have shaken each limb, I shake each branch and every twig. Then I look under every leaf."

Study of the text, without helps, was the first phase of your lesson preparation. But you can dig deeper, and there are tools to help you. The second phase of your preparation consists of using your Bible study resource books to develop that study:

Using the Study Tools

LOOK UP WORDS IN A DICTIONARY. It may surprise you to know how helpful a good dictionary can be, even in Bible study! For example, look up the following words in a regular dictionary and record their definitions.

Grace _____

_____

Blessed _____

_____

Predestinate _____

_____

READ AT LEAST ONE OTHER TRANSLATION. Sometimes an obscure word or passage can be immediately cleared up by looking at a newer translation, such as the NIV. After reading Ephesians 1:1-14 from a newer translation, write down words or phrases that have become clearer to you.

Blessed (NIV Praise) Foundation (NIV creation)
Blessings (Philips Benefits) Predestined (Planned Philips)
sealed (Philips stamped) earnest (Philips
guarantee of purchase)

EXAMINE THE CROSS-REFERENCES. For example, upon reading Ephesians 1:1, suppose you want to know what an apostle is, or what it means to be an apostle "by the will of God." The small "a" before "an apostle" in the NASB cross-reference column lists II Corinthians 1:1. Turn to this verse and locate the word "apostle." Now look in the cross-reference column to find additional references to "an apostle." Looking through these references, find Galatians 1:1. What does this verse teach you about the meaning of the word "apostle"?

An apostle is one appointed by God
not man

Looking further in Galatians 1:1, we locate the small "b" before "not." Find "b" in the cross-reference column, where it lists Galatians 1:11f. Read Galatians 1:11-24. What important things about his apostleship does Paul tell us in this passage?

Received Divine revelation for ministry
From birth a before, to reveal Christ

Helpful indeed are the cross-references in your study Bible! Now it's your turn. Locate at least two more cross-references from Ephesians 1:1-14, and show how they shed additional light on the truth of these verses. The boldfaced numbers on the far left in the cross-reference column are the verse numbers from Ephesians 1:1-14.

"heavenly places" (Eph 1:20-Realm of God)
(Eph 3:10-rulers + authorities here) (Eph 6:12-Demonic world there)
"the summing up"

"our inheritance" (Acts 26:32-shared by all saints)
(For the sanctified) It is a reward
(Eternal)

LOOK UP LOCATIONS IN A BIBLE ATLAS. Your atlas gives you a better feel for Bible land geography and its related circumstances. In Ephesians 1:1 Paul mentioned Ephesus. Locate this city in your atlas and mark its location on the map on page 44. Do you think the location of Ephesus had an effect on Paul's strategy for evangelizing the area? Why? (Compare Acts 19:10.)

A key city on the transportation routes. Helps Christianity spread

LOOK UP MEANINGS IN A BIBLE DICTIONARY. A good Bible dictionary is the place to find additional information on the many interesting topics your study will suggest to you. Use a Bible dictionary to find and record information on one or more of the following topics: Paul, apostle, saints, Ephesus, grace, predestine, adoption, mystery, redemption, blood, inheritance, seal. Write down important highlights from what you learned about this topic. Be prepared to share this information in your group discussion.

_____

_____

_____

_____

_____

_____

_____

_____

_____

_____

_____

_____

_____

CONSULT A COMMENTARY. One famous Bible teacher said that students of Scripture may fall into one of two errors. Either they will depend solely on a commentary to learn the meaning of Scripture, or they will not look at one at all. Commentaries contain a wealth of valuable information; however, they should be read near the end of your study. This way you will significantly increase your understanding of Scripture. And because you have studied it for yourself, you will be confident about sharing it with others.

Now take the commentary you have and read the section covering Ephesians 1:1-14. As you do, write down additional information and helpful insights.

_____

_____

_____

_____

_____

_____

_____

_____

Answering the Questions

With the information gathered from these six sources, you should be able to answer most or all the questions you had from the previous chapter. Briefly answer these questions here:

_____

_____

_____

_____

_____

_____

_____

_____

_____

_____

_____

_____

_____

_____

_____

_____

_____

_____

_____

_____

_____

_____

9

HEART:
APPLYING BIBLE PORTIONS

There is a form of deafness known to physicians in which the persons affected are able to hear everything except words. In such a case the ear, as an apparatus for mere hearing, may be so perfect that the tick of a watch or the song of a bird is really appreciated. But owing to a local injury deeper than the ear, in the brain itself, all spoken words are as unintelligible as those of a foreign language. Every word verbally addressed to them reaches their consciousness only as a sound, not as a word. (W. H. Thompson)

Hearing the Message

Because it is possible to have a "spiritual hearing" defect, the purpose of this lesson is not merely to gain additional information about what the Bible says or means. Rather, we are now asking: What is God saying *to me* from this passage? Am I actually *hearing* God's message to me, or are the words failing to make impact on my personal life? What lessons of guidance, encouragement, or warning do I need to hear from this passage? In other words, God's Word must go deeper than my ears; it must make contact with my heart!

The HEART aspect of learning is the key to Christian growth. It is one thing to observe, even analyze food carefully; it is quite another to accept that food, chew, and digest it, until it literally becomes a part of your body. Just so with God's Word, our spiritual food.

The purpose of this lesson then, is to help you chew and digest spiritual food more effectively—until it becomes a part of your spiritual life. *Use one of the following lists of questions to make a personal, heart application to today's Scripture passage.* For example, learn to ask questions like these when reading your Bible:

1. Is there a promise for me to claim?
2. Is there a command for me to obey?
3. Is there a sin for me to avoid?
4. Is there a principle for me to apply?

Another, more extended list of questions for devotional reading of Scripture was prepared by Terry Powell (*Welcome to the Church*: LAMP):

1. What words, phrases, or ideas are repeated in this passage? What is the significance of this repetition?

2. What commands does the passage contain? Which ones represent a timeless command for all believers? Which command speaks most personally to me? Why?

3. What can I learn from either the negative or positive examples of personalities mentioned in the passage?

4. What promises to claim can I find here?

5. What sin or shortcoming does the passage expose in my life?

6. What reasons for praising God are suggested by the content?

7. What truth or principle encourages me? Why?

8. How should what I'm reading affect my prayer life?

9. How does this passage increase my appreciation for Jesus Christ? God the Father? Or the Holy Spirit?

Still another way you may wish to apply Scripture is to ask how the passage speaks to a number of different kinds of relationships, such as:

1. Relationships in my home?
2. Relationships at work?
3. Relationships in society?

Applying the Message

Keep in mind that you may not find applications to all of these questions in a particular passage. The applications appropriate to any passage will depend on the Biblical writer's purpose and subject.

Now read Ephesians 1:1-14 devotionally. Record the personal applications you find in this passage. Be prepared to share them at the next group session.

Personal Applications _____

_____

_____

_____

_____

_____

_____

_____

_____

_____

_____

_____

_____

_____

_____

_____

_____

_____

_____

_____

_____

_____

This passage is so filled with all that God has done for us in Christ! Obviously it is not possible to find responses to all of the questions suggested, but the following are some examples of possible applications from this Scripture portion.

A PROMISE TO CLAIM: Since I have received God's grace through Christ, I can experience His peace in every area of my life.

A PRINCIPLE FOR ME TO APPLY: It is God's purpose that I should live "holy and blameless" before Him. It is not enough that I appear upright before others; He sees my heart. I pray Psalm 19:14 today.

ANOTHER PRINCIPLE TO CLAIM: It is God's purpose that my life be "to the praise of His glory"—not my own glory. In light of all God has done for me, how appropriate that my heart be filled with praise to Him!

10

HANDS:
TEACHING BIBLE PORTIONS

Dr. Howard Hendricks tells of a professor who made an impact on his life. He passed the professor's home many times, early in the morning and late at night, and often saw him pouring over his books. One day Hendricks asked him, "Doctor, I'd like to know, what is it that keeps you studying? You never cease to learn."

His answer: "Son, I would rather have my students drink from a running stream than from a stagnant pool." (*Christian Teacher*)

Regular Bible study is important. It keeps us close to the Lord, constantly finding fresh insight from His Word. But to study only for our own personal benefit is not the ultimate goal. We want to become a "running stream" of Biblical learning for others. This is the HANDS aspect of Bible study. You learned both the HEAD and the HEART aspects of Bible study in Lessons 6 through 9. You are now ready to study the HANDS approach: preparing to share Scripture truth with others—reaching out in ministry to those around you.

Preparing Bible Questions

One of the most effective ways to prepare a lesson for teaching is to make a list of questions to be used as "leading" questions in a group discussion. Not only is this usually the easiest type of Bible study to prepare, but for most people it is also the easiest to conduct.

(In addition to the leading questions for discussion, a Bible study of this type has just two other parts, both of which you can prepare without great difficulty. These are: 1] an opening, or "focusing activity" to lead into the study; 2] a comment about how you would like to close the study period. This preparation will take time. Your skills will improve as you practice preparing questions for leading Bible studies. Earnestly ask the Lord for His blessing on your preparation.)

Write down what you feel would make good questions for discussing your passage. There are several sources from which you can develop these leading questions. The first, of course, is from your own study of the passage. Looking at the questions you asked on your study work sheet is a good place to begin. Restate these questions as needed and write them below. Secondly, you may be able to add to these questions as you focus your attention on them now. Finally, devotional guides and Bible commentaries may suggest additional questions. Try to develop your own questions first, then draw from other sources only as needed.

Discussion Questions _____

_____

_____

_____

_____

_____

_____

_____

_____

_____

_____

Three Kinds of Questions to Ask

The kinds of questions you ask in your Bible study can greatly influence the quality of the discussion. The kinds of questions are parallel to the aspects of study you have been using: 1) observing the significant facts of the passage; 2) learning the meaning of these facts; and 3) applying these facts to your own life.

FACT questions draw attention to a particular verse, concept, phrase, or word that you wish to develop. These questions seek information directly from the Scripture text; they ask: what, who, when, where, why, how?

MEANING questions follow the fact question, and expand on the meaning of the passage. They focus on *interpreting* the facts and *adding more information*. Meaning questions can be answered either directly from the verse, from the context, or from appropriate cross-references. Sometimes a fuller or richer meaning can be derived from using your additional study resources.

APPLICATION questions ask: "How does this Bible truth affect my own life and that of the world around me?" In some ways this is the most important question of all.

Here are some examples from Ephesians 1, illustrating these three types of questions:

FACT QUESTION: How does Paul introduce himself in verse 1? ("an apostle")

MEANING QUESTION: What is an apostle? (See Gal. 1:1.)

APPLICATION QUESTION: Is there a sense in which God calls us to be apostles? Explain your answer.

FACT QUESTION: How does Paul describe the Ephesian Christians? ("saints," "who are faithful," "in Christ Jesus")

MEANING QUESTION: What does the word "saint" mean? (See margin: "holy one.")

APPLICATION QUESTION: In what way does Paul's description of the Ephesian Christians apply to your life?

Notice the two series of three questions focused on the same subject matter. This was by design. The meaning question is an expansion of the fact question. The application question brings out the relevance of the fact for Christian living.

Not all fact questions will lend themselves to relevant applications. You will learn to be selective in choosing fact questions with potential for helpful applications.

Before you practice using these three types of questions, look at one more example from Ephesians 1:

FACT QUESTION: Why does Paul begin this letter (after the introduction) with the joyous, "Blessed *be* the God and Father . . ."?

MEANING QUESTION: How does Paul describe the blessings we have in verse 3? ("spiritual," "in the heavenly places," "in Christ," "has blessed"—i.e., past tense)

APPLICATION QUESTION: In what ways is it important to you that these blessings are written about in the past tense? (We don't work for them; we do worship and praise God for them, as Paul did.)

As you can see, we have taken one basic fact question, brought out the meaning, and applied a part of it to our lives. Now it's your turn. Read Ephesians 1:1-14 again and note key ideas for discussion. These ideas should relate to the main idea of this passage. The main idea of Ephesians 1:1-14 is:

_____

_____

Pick out a number of important facts bearing on this main idea. Then compose questions that help develop

70

the meaning of these facts. Finally, develop other questions asking how these facts apply to our lives or circumstances as Christians. Work on these questions for at least 20 minutes before going on.

Verse _____

Fact Q _____

_____

Meaning Q _____

_____

Application Q _____

_____

Verse _____

Fact Q _____

_____

Meaning Q _____

_____

Application Q _____

_____

Verse _____

Fact Q _____

_____

Meaning Q _____

_____

Application Q _____

_____

Verse _____

Fact Q _____

_____

Meaning Q _____

Application Q _____

How did you do? If you found this difficult, take heart; experience will increase your skills in asking good questions. Although it may not be easy, developing interesting, relevant questions will bear the fruit of lively discussions! It is important that you develop your skills in asking good questions for Bible studies.

After completing your study, you may get some additonal help from studying the following examples:

VERSE 4. This passage lists a number of our God-given spiritual blessings. What is the first of these? (God chose us) When did this occur? (Before the foundation of the world) Why is this significant to us? (It shows God's wisdom; and that He took the initiative in salvation) What response should this evoke in us? (Praise and worship)

There are other ways this verse could be handled as well. Consider the following: What was God's purpose in choosing us? (That we should be holy and blameless before Him) Is this something that occurs "in Christ" or in daily practical living as well? How can this occur in greater measure in my life?

VERSES 5-8. What is the relationship we now have with God? (Adopted as sons and daughters) How did this relationship take place so far as God is concerned? (The kind intention of His will) So far as Christ is concerned? (His death) What is the appropriate response to what God has done? (We can offer our praise, and live for His praise) What else do Christians have? (Redemption) How does this occur? (Through His blood, i.e., His death) What is the result of redemption, according to verse 7? (The forgiveness of our trespasses) Notice how this was done. (vss. 7 and 8) What should be our response in light of the grace that Christ has lavished upon us? (Love, fidelity, and service to Him) (Note: You can briefly touch on the the subject of the mystery of His will, or pass over it entirely since it occupies a central place later in this epistle.)

VERSES 11-14. Why did God give us this wonderful inheritance? (That we should be "to the praise of His glory") How, do you suppose, did the Ephesian Christians understand that this would happen in their lives? How is it to occur in our lives?

This passage is so filled with the wonderful things God has done for us. Yet in v. 13 there is something we must do. What is it? (Believe) What does this word mean? (The meaning of this term can be discussed as needed) Have you made a decision to believe in Christ as your Savior?

This final section could also be handled in the following way. What happens after we hear the Gospel and believe in Christ? (We are sealed with the Holy Spirit) How is the meaning of this term brought out in verse 14? (It is a pledge of our inheritance.) Notice the last phrase in v. 14: "to the praise of His glory." A possible lesson conclusion would be: Let's close this study by thinking about ways your life can be "to the praise of His glory" this week. Share some possibilities.

NOTE: A variation of this approach may be more effective with some groups. You might simply draw attention to the fact to be discussed, briefly discuss the meaning, and give the major portion of time to the application of that meaning in life-related situations. Some groups are much more interested in discussing and applying than in merely gathering Biblical information.

Preparing the Introduction

It is fairly easy to prepare a few introductory remarks for your lesson. Your purpose is to set the stage for a free and open—yet guided—discussion of the leading lesson questions you have prepared. For example, you might introduce this first lesson in Ephesians by talking about the importance of written communication between governments or church bodies. How carefully such documents and encyclicals are often examined for their exact meaning and interpretation! Then, to move right to the Ephesians study, you might say: "As we begin this study of Paul's letter to the Ephesians we will want to give even greater attention to this inspired message from God to us."

Using your own natural friendliness, and promoting an informal atmosphere during the opening moments, will do much to set the climate for the kind of discussion which will result in profitable Bible study.

Look for a current event or other topic to use in the opening class moments—comments that will tie in with the lesson content. Use this as a bridge to turn the attention of the group to the lesson, and with it begin the lesson.

Often the best way to begin the lesson itself will be to have someone (or several) read portions of the Scripture passage to be covered.

Write the main points of how you plan to handle your introduction to the Ephesians 1:1-14 study:

_____

_____

_____

_____

_____

_____

_____

Concluding the Lesson

As with the introduction, there is no best way to conclude a Bible discussion. In fact, variety is desirable. Sometimes a summary statement will be appropriate; at other times you can use the concluding verse as an application. Sometimes one or two in the class can share the most important things that helped them; at other times it may be good to simply close in prayer. At times you might ask for a personal life response to the lesson. For example, pass out slips of paper and ask each one to write down a personal decision they are making as a result of the lesson. The special way God impressed hearts during the study will often determine its conclusion.

Record briefly your plan for concluding your Bible study on Ephesians 1:1-14.

_____

_____

_____

_____

_____

_____

Congratulations! You have now completed a Bible study which you can use to teach others! It should now be complete with an introduction; a number of fact, meaning, and application questions; and a conclusion.

11

EPHESIANS 1:15-23
STUDY A

In the next two lessons you will work through each of
the Bible study steps from Lessons 6-10, as you develop
your study of Ephesians 1:15-23. NOTE: If you plan to
lead a Bible study from this passage, you will need an
additional study time of about 1 hour to develop your
discussion questions, as taught in Lesson 10. Again,
remember to follow the five Bible study steps:

1. Pray for God's blessing, and read prayerfully.

2. Read the passage repeatedly, and thoughtfully. Try
to read the passage in at least one other translation,
such as the NIV, and note any helpful alternate readings. (Record these under "Observations.")

3. Mark and notate the text. Look first for the theme of
the passage and record this on p. 78. Now use colored
pencils to highlight important concepts. Make other
markings that will help you clarify and emphasize the
text in a way meaningful to you. During the weekly
meeting, share with others your approach to observation and marking.

4. Record your passage observations on page 79.

5. Ask the text questions. You may want to review the
suggestions for asking questions (on pages 50 and 51).
Record your questions in the space provided below.

15 For this reason I too, ªhaving heard of the faith in the Lord Jesus which *exists* among you, and ¹your love for ball the ²saints,

16 ªdo not cease giving thanks for you, bwhile making mention of *you* in my prayers;

17 that the ªGod of our Lord Jesus Christ, bthe Father of glory, may give to you a spirit of cwisdom and of drevelation in the ¹knowledge of Him.

18 *I pray that* ªthe eyes of your heart ¹may be enlightened, so that you may know what is the bhope of His ccalling, what are dthe riches of the glory of eHis inheritance in fthe ²saints,

19 and what is the surpassing greatness of His power toward us who believe. ª*These are* in accordance with the working of the bstrength of His might

20 which He brought about in Christ, when He ªraised Him from the dead, and bseated Him at His right hand in cthe heavenly *places,*

21 far above ªall rule and authority and power and dominion, and every bname that is named, not only in cthis age, but also in the one to come.

22 And He ªput all things in subjection under His feet, and gave Him as bhead over all things to the church,

23 which is His ªbody, the bfulness of Him who cfills dall in all.

---

15 ¹Many ancient mss. omit, *your love* ²Note 2, vs. 1 ªCol. 1:4; Philem. 5; Rom. 1:8 bEph. 3:18; Eph. 1:1

16 ªCol. 1:9; Rom. 1:8f. bRom. 1:9

17 ¹Or, *true knowledge* ªJohn 20:17; Rom. 15:6 bActs 7:2; 1 Cor. 2:8 cCol. 1:9 d1 Cor. 14:6

18 ¹Lit., *being* ²I.e., true believers; lit., *holy ones* ªActs 26:18; 2 Cor. 4:6; Heb. 6:4 bEph. 4:4 cRom. 11:29 dEph. 1:7 cEph. 1:11 fCol. 1:12; Acts 9:13

19 ªEph. 3:7; Phil. 3:21; Col. 1:29 bEph. 6:10

20 ªActs 2:24 bMark 16:19 cEph. 1:3

21 ªCol. 1:16; Eph. 3:10; Rom. 8:38; Matt. 28:18 bPhil. 2:9; Heb. 1:4; Rev. 19:12; John 17:11 cEph. 2:2; Matt. 12:32

22 ª1 Cor. 15:27 [fr. Ps. 8:6] bEph. 4:15; 5:23; Col. 1:18; 2:19; 1 Cor. 11:3

23 ªEph. 4:12; 5:30; Col. 1:18, 24; 2:19; 1 Cor. 12:27 bJohn 1:16; Eph. 3:19 cEph. 4:10 dCol. 3:11

Passage ___Eph 2:15 - 23___

Theme _____

_____

_____

_____

_____

_____

_____

_____

Observations

- Paul wants to know Christ better.
- Paul wants us to better understand and live in light of
    - the Christian's hope
    - the Christian's inheritance
    - the Christian's power supply.
- This reality of the Christians is the outgrowth of the great & powerful work of God ~~through~~ the death, resurrection, and exaltation of Christ
- Christ is in a position of total Lordship.
- v 19b-23 - is the heart of the book. This is what all the benefits & victories flow from.
- Paul wants us to understand that and live in light of it (which is what the rest of the ~~passage~~ book explains)
- Everything in this world & world to come is under Christ.
- The church (His body) is therefore above all things.

v. 21 What do "rule + authority + power +
dominion" refer to?

v. 18 What does this "hope" refer
to?

v. 18 Why does Paul want us to
know these things?

What is the ~~connection~~ ^{relationship} b/t
15-19a & 19b-23

Cause + Effect?

Observations:

V. 21 In rabbinic thought of 1st Century
they referred to different orders of angels.

12

EPHESIANS 1:15-23
STUDY B

This week you will complete your study of Ephesians 1:15-23. The following steps will guide your study:

Keep Studying!

1. Find at least two cross-references from this passage and indicate how they help enrich your understanding of it. Record this information under "Cross-References."

2. There are no locations to look up in a Bible atlas in this study. But keep this step in mind. It can be very helpful to know the location of the places you are studying about.

3. Look up key words from this passage in your Bible dictionary. Some words which can add to your understanding of this passage are: faith, love, wisdom, revelation, hope, inheritance and church. Briefly note significant information you find in the dictionary. Plan how you will integrate significant material in your lesson plan for teaching.

4. Read from the commentary, both for general information on these verses, and to answer your previous questions. Record brief notes of your findings under "Commentary Notes."

5. Write down applications of truth to your own heart

and life. (These applications may also be useful in leading a Bible study later.)

Observations _____

_____

_____

_____

_____

_____

_____

_____

_____

Cross-Reference Study _____

_____

_____

_____

_____

_____

_____

_____

_____

_____

_____

_____

Bible Dictionary _____

Commentary Notes _____

Personal Applications _____

For Bible Study Leaders

You will need to spend an additional hour developing key questions to ask in your Bible study. Begin by looking back to your own observations and the questions you raised while studying this passage. From those verses or passages you feel are significant, develop your own questions, beginning with fact, then meaning, and finally application. The following examples will help get you started.

FACT: What two virtues characterized the Ephesian Christians? (faith and love) What was the object of their faith? (the Lord Jesus; i.e., not merely in a Creator God, nor in their former "gods") How was their love expressed? (for all the saints)

MEANING: What correlation is there between faith and love in the Christian life?

APPLICATION: What about the person who says, "I am trusting in Christ," but does not love others?

Or take another example, based on verse 16. First ask a fact question to focus on the aspects of Paul's prayer life. (Such as: What two aspects of Paul's prayer life do you see in this verse?) The meaning of these two aspects (constancy and thanksgiving) will probably be clear to those in your study. You may wish however, to add information about these two words, either from cross-references you look up, or from a Bible dictionary. Applications readily apply to our own prayer ministry.

Work through this entire passage, developing your own fact, meaning, and application questions. You may include the ones suggested above as you wish. Record these questions on the "Lesson Plan" draft on the following pages. Then complete your lesson plan with an introduction and conclusion. You should make a final draft before teaching this lesson.

Lesson Plan (Draft)

Theme _____

_____

_____

_____

Introduction _____

_____

_____

_____

_____

_____

_____

Key Discussion Questions _____

_____

_____

_____

_____

_____

_____

_____

_____

_____

_____

_____

_____

_____

_____

_____

_____

_____

_____

_____

_____

_____

_____

_____

_____

_____

_____

_____

_____

_____

Lesson Conclusion _____

_____

_____

_____

_____

_____

NOTES: